POW

CREATED A[
BRIAN MICHAEL BEND[

COLOR ART

PETER PENTAZIS
PAT GARRAHY
BRIAN MICHAEL BENDIS

TYPOGRAPHY

KEN BRUZENAK
PAT GARRAHY
BRIAN MICHAEL BEND[

GROUPIES
CHAPTER 2

The power of a woman

A new fragrance by Jagi Jangunu

CONTROL
JAGI JANGUNU

HAMMER OF THE GODS

THREE HEROES
KICKIN' ASGARD
FOR AN EMPIRE
OF GOLD AND
THE HEART OF
AN EXOTIC
PRINCESS

JOHNNY
DEPP
KEVIN
BACON
KEVIN
SPACEY
JENNIFER
LOPEZ

An OEMING/WHEATLEY production
Co-starring BENJAMIN BRATT VANILLA ICE MICHELLE YEOH
FREDDIE PRINZE JR. & ERNEST BORGNINE as "Loki"
Music by MARSHALL MATHERS and DANNY ELFMAN
"Heroes Theme" by JOHNNY CASH
Directed by RENNY HARLIN

Soundtrack available from Def-PowersTunes

POWERS!

www.jinxworld.com

INSIDE INFORMATION

YOU'RE WATCHING....6/

IS IT ME? OR IS MELISSA RIVERS HOT?

PUNKY TODD

BRIAN MICHAEL BENDIS

FOR IMAGE COMICS
Publisher
Jim Valentino
Director of Marketing
Anthony Bozzi
Director of Production
Brent Braun
Art Director
Doug Griffith
Graphic Designer
Kenny Felix
Controller
Traci Hale

Send your letters to:
The Line Up
PO Box 14736
Cleveland, OH 44114
or email your comments to:
BRIAN1138@aol.com
or visit our website:
JINXWORLD.com

Image Comics presents POWERS
Created by BRIAN MICHAEL BENDIS & MICHAEL AVON OEMING
Coloring: PETER PANTAZIS—Lettering: KEN BRUZENAK
Copy Editor: K.C. McCRORY—Business Affairs: ALISA BENDIS

·DIARY OF THE WEEK·

Star reporter Colette McDaniel wowed the crowd with her announcement that portions of the proceeds from her new book: *Who Killed Retro Girl?* Would be going to charity (above). Hunky reporter Rogers Sanders and (Wowsa!) Weather Girl Emma Randle seem awfully chummy for co-workers (above right).

GUESS WHO CAME TO DINN

Founders of the Janis Quivers Media Center of the Arts were the brains behind the fund-raising evening at the Broderick Hotel on Benza Island, in aid of the Victims Against Random Super Powered Violence Centre.

Hosted by Channel many of the cities t came out to cook for separate tables of te each. The main ranged from jerk pizza to Sashimi salmo

'FIGHT THE MUTATION' FUNDRAISER GALA FETES SUPER STA

The applause that greeted Zora when she took the stage, in a spectacle of her trademark light, must have reminded her of the enthusiastic response she used to receive with her deceased partner, Retro Girl. But bittersweet memories did not intrude on the festivities did no on the evening's festivities.

Zora was in attendance to re

s That Be** host Ted Henry popped
h a mystery date (above top).
Washington Lee toasts the
above).

ANNUAL HERO AWARDS HONOR FG-3

Everyone had crossed fingers in hope
for the reunion to end all reunions,
but it was not to be as Wazz was a no-
show when FG-3 teammates Boggiegirl and Benmarley were awarded the
Centennial Heroes Award. The gala
event was overflowing with Dom
Perignon champagne, miniature
chocolate Award replicas, and luxury
gift baskets for all who attended.

**Awards recipients Boggiegirl and Benmarley (top) Benmarly and his
date, supermodel Roxanne Plimm (above) Boggie girl and Zora
share a hello kiss before the awards (below)**

me achievement award for her work
nst illegal mutation in our city's proj-
  The gala raised funds to enable
ren with special abilities to take part
veryday activities with regular chil-

show off

The new hammer black. Black leather. Black metallic

d the **armor** is pretty good, too

1.7 alloy VCT engine. To drive one, call 1-800-516-9226, or for more information visit www.jinxworld.com

the new ford**hammer** black

OLYMPIA DEAD
Hero found in apartment

Olympia, widely considered to be one of the city's greatest champions, was found dead Saturday night. The police have not ruled out foul play. Official reports so far indicate the police were called after a 'very bright light' burst forth from an apartment at the corner of W75th and Millar Avenue. Olympia was found in the nude, with no signs of a struggle. Police have offered very little information, but admit the case is still open and suspects are being sought for questioning. (For more information, see main article starting on page 10.)

RETRO GIRL
Vandals in mid-town

The newly erected bronze statue of Retro Girl, located in Chaykin Park was vandalized over the past weekend. The words "KAOTIC CHIC" were spray painted on it. The phrase, made popular by the man who confessed to killing Retro Girl, is now an anthem of anarchistic teen movements on the city's East Side. Police are asking citizens with any information regarding this vandalization of city property to call 443-557-8778.

FG-3
Ex-partner sues in court

The supergroup FG-3, which was recently acquitted of intimidation and bribery, charges following a nightclub battle in which three innocent bystanders were injured, is being sued for four million dollars by ex-member Wazz for royalties he says he is contractually owed for merchandising and other related commercial business ventures when he was with the group.

THIS WEEK
A ROUND-UP OF NEWS REPORTS

QUEEN NOIR
To marry ex-nemesis

Queen Noir, the celebrated cult heroine, is set to marry her one-time archenemy, Strike. The pair met during a hostage crisis at the new Federal Aviation Museum ten years ago. Strike served his time and been a reformed man for over a year and a half. Strike is the son of the late super-villain Katmandu, who died of a self-inflicted gunshot wound 17 years ago at the height of his popularity.

ZORA
Single motherhood

Zora has admitted to being a little scared of facing life as a single mother following recent news reports of her adoption of an 11-month-old girl, Katra. In an interview with the magazine *Cape*, the controversial superheroine said she was always full of admiration for single mothers, but now that she herself was one, "It was scary—a whole new path I am about to venture down."

Wazz, whose real name is Sean Wallace, claims that his former team mates Boggie girl and Benmarley have cheated him out of moneys rightfully owed to him. Wazz left the high profile group after a public argument over the death of their archenemy, Dr. Z.

A member of Wazz's legal team said: "We have no choice but to file suit. FG-3 refuses to address the issue in any other manner."

MOUNTAIN
New career name chang

In tune with new career spokesperson Coca-Cola, re ed Super Pov Mountain officially cha ed his str name to "Thi Quencher." A *Centennial Awa* winner, Mountain retired fr active status two years ago a has made a name for himself a spokesman. In a recent intervi with *TV Guide*, he stated: " are all hired monkeys. We work for as many peanuts as can. People with powers are different, and anyone who te you otherwise is a liar."

SPARKLER
Tops Powers poll

The enduri appeal of Spa ler was prov again last we when the rece ly deceased he beat out Re Girl and C queror for t title of "Most Popular Power the Century." The *Powers of Century List* was compiled by t BHC Radio2, from the votes more than 120,000 listeners. C of the list, only two, Triphamm and Zora, are still alive.

JOHNNY ROYALE
Lawsuit dropped

After months speculation, legal firm rep senting alleg organized cri boss J. "Johnn Stompinato, a.l "Johnny Roya officially dr ped its 150 million dollar la suit against the city. Though t murder of Johnny Royale is st under investigation, attorn Robert Evans said that, "furth pursuit of the legal action start by our deceased client is at th point a fruitless objective. hope that this helps the poli department find more time dedicate to our client's myst ious and violent demise."

OLYMPIA
LAST INTERVIEW:FACT vs. FICTION

EDITORIAL NOTE: **This interview was conducted two days before the sudden and tragic death of the man known as Olympia. We were going to run an edited version of this interview, but be-cause we believe that this is the last interview he ever gave, we have decided to run it in its entirety. We think this shows a rare glimpse into a man** many admired, but few knew anything about.

Also, legally, we are required to tell you that this rare interview was granted to our magazine in return for us not releasing information that fell into our possession about the man publicly known as Olympia. We will be honoring that agreement.

Olympia. Even his name conjures images of such heroism and self-lessness that immediately fills one's heart with good will towards man, he first came into our lives seven years ago, during the Denver Airport hostage situation--a situation that saved the lives of the President of Mexico and over four hundred civilians.

Olympia then went on to join The Golden Ones, a small band of self-proclaimed heroes that, singly and in groups, have successfully saved the world and mankind from plagues and perils only before imagined in the works of science fiction.

But in recent years, stories have started floating about Olympia alleged sexual transgressions. More than one young woman has come forward with stories of midnight encounters with Olympia. Shocking detail after shock-ing detail has made its way into gossip columns and TV tabloids.

►

The ***New York Times*** bestseller: *I'm With the Cape*, by self proclaimed groupie Julia Garrison, detailed a three-year affair with a man she wouldn't name by name, described as a "man of incredible power; a golden god among men," and she went on to describe intimate details of their numerous and daring encounters.

Olympia, the man, has never spoken of such matters publicly. Public opinion polls repeatedly show that most Americans don't care what our powered people do in their free time. A whopping 86 percent. But the rumors have plagued Olympia for years, and here, for the first time, he answers such questions.

POWERS: Did you read the book by Julia Garrison?

OLYMPIA: "Wow, you get right to it, don't you?"

Thought you'd appreciate that.

"And I suppose I do."

And?

"And, no, I didn't read it."

But you heard of it?

"Sure, I have a TV. I saw the press."

You have a TV?

(Laughs) "Yes, a big world exclusive. I have a TV."

So you know of the book.

"Sure."

Never even curious about what it said?

"I'll wait for the movie."

That isn't what I asked.

Good for you. Yes, I was curious, but friends of mine have read certain passages to me. It's a funny book."

Is she talking about you in the book?

"I have no idea."

Really?

"Sure. How do I know what she's doing?"

So, it could be you? You knew her?

"The entire book could be fiction for all we know. She could be having all kinds of fun making up stuff about all kinds of thoughts she's had."

So, you never met her.

"I never said that."

So, you did?

"I didn't say that, either."

Well, either you did or you didn't.

"See, I meet thousands of people every month. I could say I didn't meet her, and then it ends up I did."

But the book details an affair

"See, I meet thousands of people every month. I could say I didn't meet her, and then it ends up I did."

...hat lasted over three years.
"Wow."
And it's not with you?
"Again, I haven't read the book."
You had no affair with a woman named Julia Garrison?
"Define affair."
Are you serious?
"Sure. What's an affair? If I was having sexual relations with a woman whose name I didn't even know for over three years, I think I would have to call it something other than 'an affair.'"
What, then? What would you call it?
"I don't know. Is there a name for something like that?"
Not really.
"So there you go."
So, you may or may not have met a woman ▶

Olympia and the Golden Ones became celebrities thanks to their daring feats, but a cloud of impropriety has shadowed them, and lurid sexual innuendoes abound. Rumors of a relationship between Olympia and Retro Girl have titillated fans, particularly in the wake of the superheroine's mysterious death

"And I understand what you are trying to accomplish with this interview. But the truth of the matter is, no one cares."

named Julia Garrison, who you may or may not have had a three year relationship with, who wrote a book about someone who may or may not be you, because you didn't read it except for some of it.?

"Listen, I understand your job is hard. And I understand what you are trying to accomplish with this interview. But the truth of the matter is, no one cares. First, there's the fact that even if I had a different girlfriend every single night, and engaged in all kinds of who the hell knows what all night long, it's nobody's business. It's not illegal. It's not hurting anyone. And that's what really matters to people. So nobody cares."

Our readers care.

"No, they don't. You're trying to make them care. You want them to care in the worst way. And sure, a GOOD sex story is a good sex story, I'm not denying that. But you people run poll after poll and they tell you—'we don't care.' And I think the only reason you care is because you don't know what is going on. You don't know what the truth is, and you don't know why you can't get to it, and that bothers you."

We have a pretty good idea what the truth is.

"No, you don't. And also, I'm not an elected official. I'm just a guy who lucked into a way of life with these abilities that put me in a

position to help others. Its one of the greatest things of my life that I'm able to share that gift in a positive way. But, really, I can go on about my business not having to worry about the 'trust of the people,' or whatever.

How did you get that gift? Those powers?

(Laughs) "I can't believe you just asked for my secret origin."

Had to give it a shot.

"Ha, good for you. (Laughs) Well, that's not going to happen."

Can I ask why?

"Um—sure. A friend of mine once gave an interview just like this to a fellow like yourself, and he inadvertently gave some information that helped a ▶

Triumph and tragedy: the public life of a Super Power. Olympia has experienced the full gamut of attention in the press, from heroic adulation to pervasive intrusion during times of sorrow, and now they want to follow him into the bedroom.

ertain person bring a lot of pain
nto his life. Let's just say we've
ll learned from that."
And who was that?
I don't think I should say."
You sure?
Pretty sure."
**Some people will read this
interview and say 'there's a
man who is trying really hard
to deny yet not lie.'**
Maybe."
**There is a guy who is lying by
not telling the truth.'**
And, there are those who will say
hat this interviewer has this
hance to sit down with someone
with my unique perspective on
he world and the only questions
he is asking are sex questions."
**Maybe. Did you attend the
funeral of Retro Girl?**
No."
Why?
I didn't know where it was."
You knew her.
Yes. Great girl. One of the
best."
n the book by Julia...
Here we go—"

"You just asked for my Secret origin."

The book also describes an
affair between characters that
strongly resemble you and
Retro Girl.
"Come on, the girl is dead."
**Yes. Did you have a relation-
ship with her?**
"Yes."
Like described in the book?
"I didn't read the book, so."
**What kind of relationship did
you have?**
(Smiles) "A better one than you
and I have."
You know what I mean.
"A deaf man knows what you
mean. This—uh—isn't what we
agreed the interview would be
about."

Well...
"There's two kinds of men—men
of their word, and men who
aren't. Which are you?"
**Well, you don't seem to be
very interested in answering
questions on the subject we
did agree on discussing, so...**
"Sure I am. You're just not en-
joying the –uh—my answers."
**Actually I am, in a perverse
way. But you are avoiding the
questions that you are being
asked.**
"Define avoiding."
See?
"I was joking."
Hmmm...I wonder if you were.
"Now you sound like my thera-
pist."
Ho, you have a therapist?
"Ha! You're good."
Not going to answer?
(Olympia does not answer, but
does it with a smile.)
**Were you saddened by the
death of Retro Girl?**
"What kind of question is that?
Of course."
I didn't mean anything ▶

by it. It's just a **direct question.**
"Lord..."

I thought if I asked you how you felt when you learned of it, that would be more vague and not to your liking.
"Uh-huh. Well, for your information, the whole thing was devastating to me. The death, the whole thing with Triphammer. There were no winners in that terrible story. If you notice, I wasn't around for a while after that. It took a lot out for me to put on my uniform after that..."

Why?
"Just questioning why we do what we do. Is it worth it? Do we make a difference?

And?
"And I think we do. I think we do in a big way. And though that dark chapter in our city's histo will always be there, I just—"(I is visibly shaken by the subject.)

Do you want to continue?
(Pauses) "Uh--not really. T you what? You and your mag zine can run whatever you wa I don't care. I have no regre about my life or how I condu myself. My relationships are n own. My friends know who th

re. I love this city and the peo-ple in it, and the love I get back rom them is the greatest gift I ould ever hope for. The women n my life are all...

The thing is—you couldn't possibly understand the needs of eople like myself. Our appetites, ur desires. You couldn't possibly nderstand the special relation-hips someone like myself could

have with certain women who do understand just what we're about. Women who just want to show their appreciation to us for our dedication and hard work. And even if you could understand it--- what difference would it make? Would it make me a worse per-son? Would it take back any of the sacrifices I've made, or...?

"Just—just print whatever the

hell you want. There's someone out there who needs me right now."

(Olympia flies away.)

F

INTERVIEW: MIKE SANGIACOMO
PHOTOS: AVON ARCHIVES
© POWERS! MAGAZINE
WORLDS RIGHTS RESERVED

IN MEMORIAM
OLYMPIA

GROUPIES
CHAPTER 3

RIDE ALONG

NOT A COP.

NOT A COP.

WILL YOU SHUT UP?

I'M A WRITER.

A WRITER?

REPORTER?

NO.

NO?

GRAPHIC NOVELS.

YEAH?

AND WHAT THE FUCK ARE YOU DOING HERE IN THE MIDDLE OF WHERE YOU DON'T BELONG?

RESEARCH.

SHUT UP! DO YOU EVER SHUT UP??!!

RESEARCH?

OH, LIKE A RIDE-ALONG.

I DIDN'T KNOW YOU GUYS ACTUALLY DID THAT?

I THOUGHT YOU MADE IT UP SO YOU SOUNDED COOL AND ALL AUTHENTIC.

SOME TIMES WE DO YEAH

THE SHARK

CLICKCLICKCLICKCLUCK

MA'AM, DO YOU THINK YOU COULD *DESCRIBE* THE OTHER GENTLEMAN THAT WAS HERE?

THE *CAUCASIAN* FELLOW?

! GUESS.

GOOD. LET'S...

HE PAID WITH A CREDIT CARD.

DOES THAT HELP YOU?

! HAVE THE RECEIPT IN THE REGISTER...

BACK IN THE GAME?

WHAT GAME?

BUT THE THING IS-- IS THAT HE TURNED ON ME.

NO!!!

YES.

HE STARTED HITTING ME WITH HIS STAFF, AND I TOLD HIM I WAS STRONGER THAN HIM AND TO CUT IT OUT.

AT FIRST, I THOUGHT HE WAS KIDDING BUT HE WAS TOTALLY TURNING ON ME.

AND I PUSHED HIM-- HARDER THAN I MEANT TO--

--AND--AND HE SLIPPED.

END

PARTIAL TRANSCRIPT FROM COURT DOCKET 55673-2433

THE PEOPLE VS. GRIFFIN MILLS.

APPEARANCES:

For Plaintiff:

Attorney CLIVE BARROW

For Defendant:

NICHOLAS CORIC District Attorney

JULIET PECK Assistant District Attorney

CSR# 45564

OFFICIAL REPORTER ROBERT STRICT

DATED October 25, 2001   COURTROOM 4

CC: THIS PUPPY OVER TO A DET. DEENA PILGRIM OVER AT HOMICIDE S™ PR. POWERS DIV.

I have the drawings from Channel 5 too - send them as well?

(CONTINUED

CONTINUED:

COURT RESUMES. 10:11 am October 22, 2001

          DEFENSE ATTORNEY CLIVE BARROW
THE DEFENSE WOULD LIKE TO CALL TO THE
STAND... MR. THOMAS MILLS.

DEFENDANT THOMAS MILLS TAKES THE STAND. THE BAILIFF
APPROACHES.

          BAILIFF
DO YOU SWEAR TO TELL THE TRUTH, THE WHOLE
TRUTH, AND NOTHING BUT THE TRUTH, SO HELP
YOU GOD?

          TOMMY MILLS
YES. YES, I DO.

          BAILIFF
YOU MAY SIT.

DEFENSE ATTORNEY CLIVE BARROW APPROACHES.

          DEFENSE ATTORNEY CLIVE BARROW
THOMAS...

          TOMMY MILLS
TOMMY IS OK?

          DEFENSE ATTORNEY CLIVE BARROW
TOMMY, TELL THE COURT HOW YOU CAME TO
HAVE POWERS?

          TOMMY MILLS
WELL, IN COLLEGE I WAS WORKING A- A
SUMMER CONSTRUCTION JOB. JUST MANUAL
STUFF. WE WERE MAKING ROOM FOR THIS RIG-
DIGGING. CLEARING AN AREA OUT FOR IT. AND
ONE OF THE GUYS HIT ONE OF THE
UNDERGROUND PIPES- OR WE THOUGHT IT WAS A
PIPE, BUT IT WAS ACTUALLY THIS METAL
CANISTER OF SOME KIND. AND WHEN THE GUY-
SCOTTY- WHEN HE HIT IT WITH HIS SHOVEL-
THIS GAS CAME SEEPING OUT. IT WAS FULL OF
THIS BLUEISH GAS. AND EVERYONE AROUND ME.
WE- WE ALL STARTED CHOKING. I FAINTED. I
NEVER DID THAT BEFORE, BUT I FAINTED. I
WAS HOLDING MY EYES. AND WHEN I WOKE UP
IN THE HOSPITAL, THEY TOLD ME THAT
EVERYONE ELSE AT THE SITE HAD DIED.
EVERYONE EXCEPT FOR ME.

          DEFENSE ATTORNEY CLIVE BARROW
A BLUE-ISH GAS.

          (CONTINUED

CONTINUED: (2)

                    TOMMY MILLS
          YES.

                    DEFENSE ATTORNEY CLIVE BARROW
          DID YOU EVER FIND OUT WHAT THE GAS WAS?

                    TOMMY MILLS
          NO, NO BUT I ASKED AROUND. I ASKED THE
          CONSTRUCTION COMPANY I WORKED FOR BUT
          THEY SAID THEY DIDN'T KNOW. SOMEONE TOLD
          ME SOMETHING ABOUT THE F.B.I. BEING
          INVOLVED, BUT I DON'T REALLY KNOW
          ANYTHING BEYOND THAT.

                    PROSECUTOR CORIC
          OBJECTION.

                    JUDGE ROLLINS
          SUSTAINED.

                    DEFENSE ATTORNEY CLIVE BARROW
          HOW MANY PEOPLE DIED IN THE ACCIDENT,
          TOMMY?

                    TOMMY MILLS
          UH- TEN. TEN.

                    DEFENSE ATTORNEY CLIVE BARROW
          AND YOU WERE THE SOLE SURVIVOR?

                    TOMMY MILLS
          WELL, SOME OTHER GUYS RAN AWAY BEFORE THE
          GAS REACHED THEM, BUT I WAS THE ONLY ONE
          IN THE IMMEDIATE AREA. YEAH, IT WAS
          REALLY SAD.

                    DEFENSE ATTORNEY CLIVE BARROW
          THE SOLE SURVIVOR.

                    TOMMY MILLS
          I DON'T KNOW WHY? BUT YEAH, I GUESS.

                    DEFENSE ATTORNEY CLIVE BARROW
          AND WHEN YOU RECOVERED YOU FOUND THAT YOU
          HAD POWERS.

                    TOMMY MILLS
          YES, SIR.

                    DEFENSE ATTORNEY CLIVE BARROW
          WHAT POWERS DO YOU HAVE, TOMMY?

                    TOMMY MILLS
          I HAVE - WELL, I'M PRETTY STRONG AND I
          CAN JUMP REALLY HIGH. CAN'T FLY, JUST
          JUMP. AND I'M PRETTY FAST NOW, AND MY
          SKIN IS- IT DOESN'T BREAK THAT EASILY.
          AND MY EYE SIGHT. ALL MY SENSES REALLY-
          THEY'RE REALLY STRONG. I REGISTERED IN AT
          LEVEL FIVE.

                    DEFENSE ATTORNEY CLIVE BARROW
          AND WHEN YOU FOUND YOU HAD THESE POWERS,
          WHAT DID YOU DO?

                    TOMMY MILLS
          I- WELL, IT WAS KIND OF FATE REALLY,
          BECAUSE THAT SAME WEEK I HAPPENED TO WALK
          INTO A CONVENIENT STORE THAN WAS BEING
          HELD UP AND I - I WAS ABLE TO STOP THE
          BURGLARY. NO ONE WAS HURT. IT- IT WAS A
          GOOD FEELING.

                    DEFENSE ATTORNEY CLIVE BARROW
          WOW.

                    TOMMY MILLS
          AND I REALIZED THAT I- I HAD A CALLING-
          THAT I WAS REALLY LUCKY.

                    DEFENSE ATTORNEY CLIVE BARROW
          INDEED.

                    TOMMY MILLS
          SO, I REGISTERED MY COSTUME, GAVE MYSELF
          A NAME.

                    DEFENSE ATTORNEY CLIVE BARROW
          'METEOR?'

                    TOMMY MILLS
          METEOR.

                    DEFENSE ATTORNEY CLIVE BARROW
          WHY METEOR?

                    TOMMY MILLS
          THOUGHT IT SOUNDED PRETTY COOL.

COURTROOM SNICKERS. JUDGE HITS THE GAVEL.

                    JUDGE ROLLINS
          ORDER.

                                        (CONTINUED

CONTINUED: (4)

                    TOMMY MILLS
          WELL, I-I-I DID.

                    DEFENSE ATTORNEY CLIVE BARROW
          YOU HAD A PRETTY STRONG START WITH YOUR
          NEW CAREER. A COUPLE OF COLORFUL DISPLAYS
          OF HEROISM.

                    TOMMY MILLS
          YES, SIR.

                    DEFENSE ATTORNEY CLIVE BARROW
          YOU SAVED THAT GIRL IN THE PARK.

                    TOMMY MILLS
          YES, SIR.

                    DEFENSE ATTORNEY CLIVE BARROW
          POWERS MAGAZINE FEATURED YOU IN THEIR 'ON
          THE RISE' SIDE BAR

                    TOMMY MILLS
          YES, SIR.

                    DEFENSE ATTORNEY CLIVE BARROW
          BUT YOU KIND OF FELL OUT OF THE SPOTLIGHT
          AFTER THAT...

                    TOMMY MILLS
          YES, SIR.

                    DEFENSE ATTORNEY CLIVE BARROW
          WHAT HAPPENED? WHERE'D YOU GO?

                    TOMMY MILLS
          WELL, I WAS STILL PRETTY NEW AT ALL OF
          IT, AND I DIDN'T UNDERSTAND, REALLY, HOW
          THE MEDIA WORKED. SO WHEN I WAS ASKED BY
          THIS MAGAZINE SOMETHING ABOUT A POWERED
          PERSONS RESPONSIBILITY IN OUR SOCIETY AND
          IF IT WAS GOOD FOR THE CITY- WELL, I HAD
          MY QUOTE TAKEN OUT OF CONTEXT AND-

                    DEFENSE ATTORNEY CLIVE BARROW
          WHAT DID YOU SAY?

                    TOMMY MILLS
          I SAID THAT I THOUGHT IT WAS GOOD FOR THE
          CITY TO HAVE PEOPLE WHO WERE WILLING TO
          BE WHERE THE COPS WEREN'T ABLE TO BE OR
          COULDN'T BE. BUT IN THE ARTICLE IT
          SOUNDED WRONG.
                         (MORE)

6

                    TOMMY MILLS (CONT'D)
IT SOUNDED IN THE ARTICLE AS IF I THOUGHT
SUPER POWERED PEOPLE WERE DOING THE COPS
JOB FOR THEM. THE TONE OF THE PIECE, IT-
IT WASN'T WHAT I WAS TOLD IT WAS GOING TO
BE.

                    DEFENSE ATTORNEY CLIVE BARROW
AND WHERE DID THIS ARTICLE RUN?

                    TOMMY MILLS
IN AIR MAGAZINE.

                    DEFENSE ATTORNEY CLIVE BARROW
YOU THINK THE COMMENTS WERE TAKEN OUT OF
CONTEXT?

                    TOMMY MILLS
OH, DEFINITELY. I WASN'T SLAMMING THE
COPS. I ADMIRE THE COPS. I- I WAS TRYING
TO SAY SOMETHING POSITIVE. I THOUGHT IT
WAS NICE THAT WE HAVE THE COPS PLUS WE
ALSO HAVE PEOPLE WHO ARE WILLING TO DRESS
UP AND SYMBOLIZE SOMETHING AND BE
PROACTIVE IN THE COMMUNITY.

                    DEFENSE ATTORNEY CLIVE BARROW
'PROACTIVE IN THE COMMUNITY.' WELL SAID.

                    TOMMY MILLS
THANKS, WELL, THIS- THIS ARTICLE WAS LIKE
A DEATH RATTLE FOR MY CAREER AS A SUPER
HERO. ALL THE COPS PUT ME ON THEIR SHIT
LIST OR SOMETHING. EXCUSE MY LANGUAGE. I-
I COULDN'T CATCH A BREAK AFTER THE
ARTICLE. IT WAS WEIRD.

                    DEFENSE ATTORNEY CLIVE BARROW
HOW SO?

                    TOMMY MILLS
THE COPS- THE POLICE WOULD IGNORE ME WHEN
THEY SHOWED UP. WHICH IS FINE, I GUESS. I
MEAN, THEY CERTAINLY DON'T OWE ME
ANYTHING. OR- YEAH- OR THEY WOULD TAKE
THE GUY I CAUGHT FOR THEM AND BOOK HIM
WITHOUT GIVING ME ANY CREDIT IN THE
REPORT. AND IN SOME INSTANCES THEY WOULD
JUST LET THE GUY GO. JUST LET HIM GO
RIGHT IN FRONT OF ME.

                    PROSECUTOR CORIC
OBJECTION. MOVE TO STRIKE.

                    JUDGE ROLLINS
SUSTAINED. COUNSELLOR? ROUND IT HOME.

                    DEFENSE ATTORNEY CLIVE BARROW
SO YOU FELT YOUR ACTIONS WERE...?

                    TOMMY MILLS
I WAS TRYING TO BE HELPFUL. I WAS TRYING
TO BE PART OF THE COMMUNITY- BUT ITS HARD
WHEN THE COMMUNITY IS GIVING YOU THE COLD
SHOULDER. WHEN THE LAW ENFORCEMENT
OFFICIALS WERE-

                    PROSECUTOR CORIC
OBJECTION.

                    JUDGE ROLLINS
SUSTAINED. MOVE FORWARD ON THIS.

                    TOMMY MILLS
WELL, IT- IT WAS MADE VERY CLEAR AFTER
THAT ARTICLE THAT THERE WAS LITTLE OR NO
NEED FOR 'METEOR.' I KNOW WHEN I'M NOT
WANTED.

                    DEFENSE ATTORNEY CLIVE BARROW
WHAT DID YOU DO?

                    TOMMY MILLS
I TOOK THE HINT AND I - I WENT BACK TO MY
NORMAL LIFE. CIVILIAN LIFE.

                    DEFENSE ATTORNEY CLIVE BARROW
TELL ME HOW YOU MET REGINALD COPPER WHO
WE NOW KNOW PUBLICLY AS T.R.K.

                    TOMMY MILLS
BEFORE I RETIRED, HE TRIED TO ROB THE
NOZAMACK JEWELRY STORE.

                    DEFENSE ATTORNEY CLIVE BARROW
THE ONE DOWNTOWN?

                    TOMMY MILLS
YES. AND I GOT TO HIM BEFORE HE DID ANY
REAL DAMAGE OR GOT AWAY.

                    DEFENSE ATTORNEY CLIVE BARROW
AND HE WENT TO JAIL BECAUSE OF THIS.
BECAUSE OF YOU'RE TIMELY EFFORTS.

                    TOMMY MILLS
YES.

                    DEFENSE ATTORNEY CLIVE BARROW
AND YOU WERE IN CONTACT WITH HIM AFTER
THAT?

              TOMMY MILLS
YES, WE CORRESPONDED.

                    DEFENSE ATTORNEY CLIVE BARROW
BY MAIL.

              TOMMY MILLS
YES. HE TOLD ME IT WAS PART OF A PROGRAM
IN THE PRISON. A PRISON PROGRAM. THE
PRIEST TOLD HIM TO BREAK DOWN THE WALL
BETWEEN WHERE HE WAS AND HOW HE GOT HERE.

                    DEFENSE ATTORNEY CLIVE BARROW
AND YOU RESPONDED?

              TOMMY MILLS
YES, IT WAS A HEARTFELT LETTER AND I FELT
WE ACTUALLY HAD A LOT IN COMMON. IT
SEEMED LIKE THE RIGHT THING TO DO.

                    DEFENSE ATTORNEY CLIVE BARROW
AND HE FOUND YOU, HOW?

              TOMMY MILLS
I ASSUMED HE LOOKED IT UP IN THE BOOK. I-
I REALLY DIDN'T SEE THE REASON FOR A
SECRET IDENTITY.

                    DEFENSE ATTORNEY CLIVE BARROW
WHY NOT?

              TOMMY MILLS
THEY ALWAYS SEEMED TO ME TO BE KIND OF
LIKE LYING. LYING AND HIDING. JUST DIDN'T
OCCUR TO ME TO DO THAT.

                    DEFENSE ATTORNEY CLIVE BARROW
AND YOU KEPT THIS UP- THIS CORRESPONDENCE
FOR THE ENTIRE NINE YEARS HE WAS IN
PRISON.

              TOMMY MILLS
YES. ON AND OFF. BUT YES.

                    DEFENSE ATTORNEY CLIVE BARROW
SO, YOU WERE FRIENDS?

              TOMMY MILLS
I THOUGHT SO, YES.

                                        (CONTINUED

                    DEFENSE ATTORNEY CLIVE BARROW
AND IN ALL THAT TIME DID HE EVER TELL YOU
THAT HE PLANNED ON ROBBING AGAIN WHEN HE
GOT OUT?

                    TOMMY MILLS
NO, SIR. NO.

                    DEFENSE ATTORNEY CLIVE BARROW
HE DIDN'T?

                    TOMMY MILLS
NO, NO I WOULD HAVE ENDED THE
CORRESPONDENCE IMMEDIATELY IF THAT HAD
HAPPENED.

                    DEFENSE ATTORNEY CLIVE BARROW
DID YOU EVER TALK ABOUT IT IN THE
HYPOTHETICAL?

                    TOMMY MILLS
NO. NEVER. HE ONLY BROUGHT UP HIS PAST IN
THE CONTEXT OF HIS TALKS WITH THE PRIEST.
HE ALWAYS SOUNDED VERY REMORSEFUL.
ALWAYS.

                    DEFENSE ATTORNEY CLIVE BARROW
AND WHEN HE GOT OUT OF JAIL, YOU SAW EACH
OTHER SOCIALLY?

                    TOMMY MILLS
ONLY A COUPLE OF TIMES. HE WAS ONLY OUT A
FEW MONTHS.

                    DEFENSE ATTORNEY CLIVE BARROW
WHAT DID YOU TALK ABOUT WHEN YOU GOT
TOGETHER?

                    TOMMY MILLS
WELL, LOTS OF STUFF. MOVIES, GIRLS. BUT
WE TALKED A LOT ABOUT HOW HARD IT WAS FOR
HIM TO READJUST TO CIVILIAN LIFE.

                    DEFENSE ATTORNEY CLIVE BARROW
AND WAS IT DURING THESE TALKS THAT HE
BROUGHT UP THE IDEA OF ROBBING THE-

                    PROSECUTOR CORIC
OBJECTION. LEADING.

                    JUDGE ROLLINS
SUSTAINED. CONTINUE.

                    DEFENSE ATTORNEY CLIVE BARROW
WHEN WAS THE FIRST TIME REGINALD BROUGHT
UP THE IDEA OF THE ROBBERY?

                    TOMMY MILLS
THAT DAY. THE DAY HE- HE DIED.

                    DEFENSE ATTORNEY CLIVE BARROW
HOW DID IT COME UP?

                    TOMMY MILLS
HE STARTED TALKING ABOUT HOW RESTLESS HE
FELT BEING OUT OF 'THE GAME' AND THE
GLORY DAYS AND ALL THAT. YOU KNOW?

                    DEFENSE ATTORNEY CLIVE BARROW
UH HUH.

                    TOMMY MILLS
HE SAID HE HAD AN IDEA TO START FRESH. HE
SAID WE- WE NEEDED SOMETHING LIKE THAT
SUMMER OF '89 TO REALLY PUT US ON THE MAP
AGAIN. TO GET EVERYONE'S ATTENTION. HE
SAID HE WAS GOING TO DO THE ROBBERY AND
THAT I SHOULD TRY TO BREAK IT UP, BUT LET
HIM GET AWAY JUST IN THE NICK OF TIME. HE
SAID WE'D BOTH MAKE THE PAPER. I COULDN'T
BELIEVE WHAT HE WAS SAYING.

                    DEFENSE ATTORNEY CLIVE BARROW
AND WHAT DID YOU SAY?

                    TOMMY MILLS
AT FIRST, I THOUGHT HE WAS JOKING. HE- IT
WAS SO UNLIKE HIM. IT WAS ONLY AFTER HE
STARTED TALKING THIS WAY THAT I REALIZED
THAT HE MIGHT HAVE BEEN DRINKING. HE WAS
QUITE IRRATIONAL AND VERY UNLIKE HIMSELF-
EDGY. AND I - AND I FELT BAD FOR HIM
BECAUSE I KNEW HOW HARD HE HAD TRIED TO
GET HIS LIFE TOGETHER, BUT AT THE SAME
TIME- I WAS, WELL, OVERWHELMED WITH A
FEELING OF DISGUST AND BETRAYAL THAT MY
FRIEND- THIS PERSON I THOUGHT WAS MY
FRIEND- WOULD NOW SOMEHOW TRY TO INVOLVE
ME IN THIS.

                    DEFENSE ATTORNEY CLIVE BARROW
SO, YOU TOLD HIM NO.

                    TOMMY MILLS
I DID, THEN I PAID THE BILL, GOT UP, AND
I WALKED OUT OF THE DINER.

                                        (CONTINUED

CONTINUED: (10)

                    DEFENSE ATTORNEY CLIVE BARROW
BUT YOU CAME BACK.

                         TOMMY MILLS
IT- IT WAS VERY CLEAR THAT I HAD TO STOP
HIM. THAT I HAD TO COME BACK INTO 'THE
GAME' AND STOP HIM.

                    DEFENSE ATTORNEY CLIVE BARROW
WHY DIDN'T YOU CALL THE POLICE?

                         TOMMY MILLS
I DID.

                    DEFENSE ATTORNEY CLIVE BARROW
YOU DID?

                         TOMMY MILLS
I DID. BUT THEY SAID SQUAD CARS WERE
ALREADY ON THE WAY THERE. THEY SAID HE
CALLED IT IN- DARED THEM, TO COME GET
HIM.

                    DEFENSE ATTORNEY CLIVE BARROW
SO WHY DIDN'T YOU JUST STAY HOME?

                         TOMMY MILLS
I COULDN'T- I KNEW WHAT HE COULD DO TO
THE POLICE OFFICERS. I KNEW WHAT HIS
WEAPONRY COULD DO TO THEM IF THEY WEREN'T
PREPARED. AND I COULD GET THERE IN NO
TIME AT ALL. I FELT A RESPONSIBILITY. TEN
YEARS. HE WAS MY FRIEND.

                    DEFENSE ATTORNEY CLIVE BARROW
AND WHEN YOU GOT THERE...

                         TOMMY MILLS
HE SAID HE KNEW I WOULD COME, THAT I
WOULDN'T LET HIM DOWN. I TOLD HIM- I SAID
I WASN'T THERE TO HELP. I WAS THERE TO
STOP HIM BEFORE THINGS GOT OUT OF HAND.
BUT HE STARTED LAUGHING AND SWINGING
WILDLY. HE- HE -HE JUST WENT MANIC ON ME.

                    DEFENSE ATTORNEY CLIVE BARROW
AND THAT'S WHEN HE SLIPPED.

                         TOMMY MILLS
THAT'S WHEN HE SLIPPED.

              DEFENSE ATTORNEY CLIVE BARROW
IN YOUR OPINION, WAS THERE ANYWAY FOR YOU
TO SAVE HIM?

              TOMMY MILLS
DON'T YOU THINK I WOULD HAVE IF I COULD?

              DEFENSE ATTORNEY CLIVE BARROW
NO FURTHER QUESTIONS.

ROSECUTOR CORIC APPROACHES.

              PROSECUTOR CORIC
MR. MILLS, YOU TOLD THE DETECTIVES WHO
QUESTIONED AND THEN ARRESTED YOU FOR
MURDER THAT YOU WERE NOT IN THE DINER
THAT NIGHT. YOU HELD TO THAT STORY UNTIL
THEY COULD PROVE TO YOU THAT YOU WERE
THERE WITH A CREDIT CARD RECEIPT. AND NOW
YOU SAY YOU WERE THERE- BUT THAT YOU
QUICKLY LEFT AFTER YOU FOUND OUT THE
DECEASED HAD A DASTARDLY PLAN.

              TOMMY MILLS
YES.

              PROSECUTOR CORIC
SO AFTER YOUR FRIEND BETRAYED YOUR TRUST
AND ADMITTED TO YOU WHAT HIS INTENTIONS
WERE- YOU STOPPED AND BOUGHT HIM DINNER?

              TOMMY MILLS
I-

              PROSECUTOR CORIC
YOU DIDN'T JUST WALK RIGHT OUT AND LEAVE
IN A HUFF. YOU FELT COMPELLED TO SAY:
I'LL GET THIS ONE?

              TOMMY MILLS
I-

              PROSECUTOR CORIC
YES?

              TOMMY MILLS
I JUST DID.

              PROSECUTOR CORIC
MR. MILLS, IN THIS TEN YEARS OF
CORRESPONDENCE WITH THE DECEASED DID YOU
EVER KEEP ANY OF THE LETTERS?

(CONTINUED

                    TOMMY MILLS
     NO.

                    PROSECUTOR CORIC
     NO?

                    TOMMY MILLS
     NO.

                    PROSECUTOR CORIC
     WHY NOT?

                    TOMMY MILLS
     I'M KIND OF A NEAT FREAK. DON'T LIKE-
     DON'T LIKE A LOT OF CLUTTER.

                    PROSECUTOR CORIC
     WOULD IT SURPRISE YOU TO FIND OUT THAT
     THE DECEASED, IN FACT, DID?

                    TOMMY MILLS
     WHAT?

               DEFENSE ATTORNEY CLIVE BARROW
     OBJECTION YOUR HONOR!

                    PROSECUTOR CORIC
     YOUR HONOR I WOULD LIKE TO ENTER INTO
     EVIDENCE THIS LOVELY CASE- FULL OF THE
     ACTUAL HANDWRITTEN CORRESPONDENCE BETWEEN
     THE DEFENDANT AND THE DECEASED AND I
     WOULD LIKE TO ENTER IT AS STATES EVIDENCE
     C.

               DEFENSE ATTORNEY CLIVE BARROW
     OBJECTION!

                    JUDGE ROLLINS
     OVERRULED.

                    TOMMY MILLS
     WHAT IS GOING- ?

                    PROSECUTOR CORIC
     IS THIS YOUR HANDWRITING, SIR?

                    TOMMY MILLS
     I DON'T KNOW.

                    PROSECUTOR CORIC
     DID YOU WRITE THIS?

CONTINUED: (13)

                    TOMMY MILLS
          I DON'T KNOW.

                    PROSECUTOR CORIC
          YOU DON'T KNOW? WELL, THAT'S OK, WE CAN
          GET A HANDWRITING EXPERT IN HERE IN A FEW
          MINUTES WHO WILL GLADLY TESTIFY THAT IT
          IS, IN FACT, YOUR VERY OWN HANDWRITING.
          WOULD YOU LIKE A CLOSER LOOK?

                    TOMMY MILLS
          NO.

                    PROSECUTOR CORIC
          NO? WOW, IF I WAS ON TRIAL FOR MURDER AND
          THE PROSECUTOR JUST SHOVED A PIECE OF
          PAPER IN MY FACE WHILE I WAS ON THE
          STAND... I WOULD WANT A CLOSER LOOK. BUT
          THAT'S ME. I'M A FREAK.

                    TOMMY MILLS
          IT MIGHT BE MINE.

                    PROSECUTOR CORIC
          'MIGHT BE?'

                    TOMMY MILLS
          ITS HARD TO SAY.

                    PROSECUTOR CORIC
          WELL, READ FOR ME THE HIGHLIGHTED AREA ON
          THIS ONE HERE. SEE IF IT RINGS ANY BELLS
          FOR YOU. THIS ONE IS DATED 2 YEARS AND 3
          MONTHS AGO. READ HERE. YOUR HONOR?

                    JUDGE ROLLINS
          MR. MILLS, PLEASE DO WHAT THE PROSECUTOR
          ASKS.

                    TOMMY MILLS
          'DEAR REG, UCHUM- I- UH- I WAS REALLY
          GLAD YOU WROTE BACK TO ME. I BET YOU WERE
          SHOCKED TO-'

                    PROSECUTOR CORIC
          LOUDER, MR. MILLS.

                    TOMMY MILLS
          'I BET YOU WERE SHOCKED TO HEAR FROM ME,
          OF ALL PEOPLE, OUT OF THE BLUE. I HAD A
          REALLY SHITTY WEEK THIS WEEK.
                         (MORE)

(CONTINUED

                    TOMMY MILLS (CONT'D)
I KIND OF FEEL FUNNY BITCHING ABOUT MY
LIFE CONSIDERING YOUR SITUATION, BUT IT'S
REALLY NOT SO EASY ON THE OUTSIDE WORLD.
I HAVE THIS MENIAL JOB, YET I HAVE ALL
THESE THINGS- THESE POWERS I COULD- UH-
DO. WHEN I THINK OF ALL THOSE UNTALENTED
HACKS WITH ALL THOSE MERCHANDISING DEALS.
AND HERE I AM SITTING IN A CUBICLE HOPING
MY BITCH OF A BOSS DOESN'T BITCH AT ME.
WE GOT FIND A WAY TO... GET BACK IN THE
GAME. I DON'T KNOW ABOUT YOU... BUT I
JUST HAVE TO. ANY IDEAS?'

                    PROSECUTOR CORIC
DID YOU WRITE THAT?

                    TOMMY MILLS
MAYBE.

                    PROSECUTOR CORIC
WELL MR. MILLS, WE WILL HAVE THE
TESTIMONY FROM THE HANDWRITING EXPERT IN
A MINUTE. I HAVE ANOTHER QUESTION: YOU
TOLD THE ARRESTING DETECTIVES THAT THE
DECEASED CONTACTED YOU FROM JAIL FIRST.
THAT HE MADE FIRST CONTACT. WHICH IS IT?

                    TOMMY MILLS
WHAT- WHAT I SAID TODAY-

                    PROSECUTOR CORIC
'WHAT YOU SAID TODAY' WHAT?

                    TOMMY MILLS
WHAT I SAID TODAY- THAT- THAT IS THE
TRUTH.

                    PROSECUTOR CORIC
WILL IT BE THE TRUTH TOMORROW? OR IS WHAT
YOU SAY ONLY TRUE FOR THE DAY...

                    TOMMY MILLS
I...

                    DEFENSE ATTORNEY CLIVE BARROW
OBJECTION!

                    PROSECUTOR CORIC
STRIKE. MR. MILLS, IF, IN FACT, YOU HAD
NO IDEA THAT YOU WERE GOING TO BE GETTING
BACK INTO 'THE GAME' AS YOU SO ELOQUENTLY
COMPLAIN ABOUT IN YOUR MANY, MANY LETTERS
TO YOUR IMPRISONED FRIEND- WHO WAS, IN
FACT, ONCE YOUR ENEMY...
                    (MORE)

CONTINUED: (15)

PROSECUTOR CORIC (CONT'D)
HOW IS IT THAT YOU HAD A NEW IDENTITY AND
COSTUME ALL READY TO GO?

TOMMY MILLS
I DIDN'T SAY-

PROSECUTOR CORIC
WHAT?

TOMMY MILLS
I DIDN'T SAY I DIDN'T WANT TO GET BACK
INTO 'THE GAME,' I SAID I -

PROSECUTOR CORIC
PLEASE ANSWER THE QUESTION YOU WERE
ASKED.

TOMMY MILLS
I JUST HAD IT.

PROSECUTOR CORIC
'YOU JUST HAD IT?' WOW. YOU JUST HAD A
2000 DOLLAR COSTUME MADE. JUST HAPPENED
TO HAVE IT.

TOMMY MILLS
NO COMMENT.

PROSECUTOR CORIC
NO COMMENT? THIS ISN'T A PRESS
CONFERENCE. SIR, THIS IS A COURT OF LAW
AND YOU ARE UNDER OATH.

TOMMY MILLS
I...

PROSECUTOR CORIC
IT'S OK MR. MILLS. I THINK YOU ANSWERED
THE QUESTION QUITE CLEARLY. I'LL PUT THAT
ANSWER INTO THE GIANT HOLE IN YOUR STORY
ALONG WITH THE REST OF THEM.

DEFENSE ATTORNEY CLIVE BARROW
OBJECTION.

PROSECUTOR CORIC
NO FURTHER QUESTIONS.

DEFENSE ATTORNEY CLIVE BARROW APPROACHES.

DEFENSE ATTORNEY CLIVE BARROW
TOMMY, WHEN YOU WERE BEING QUESTIONED BY
THE POLICE WERE YOU UNDER WHAT THEY CALL:
A DRAINER?

                    TOMMY MILLS
          YES, OH YEAH- YES.

                    DEFENSE ATTORNEY CLIVE BARROW
          WAS IT HARD FOR YOU TO THINK UNDER THE
          DRAINER?

                    PROSECUTOR CORIC
          OBJECTION.

                    JUDGE ROLLINS
          OVERRULED.

                    DEFENSE ATTORNEY CLIVE BARROW
          DID YOU COMPLAIN TO THE DETECTIVES THAT
          THE DRAINER WAS MAKING IT HARD TO THINK?

                    TOMMY MILLS
          YES, YES I DID. I TOLD THEM THAT I FELT
          ACHY AND NAUSEOUS, BUT THEY IGNORED ME.

                    DEFENSE ATTORNEY CLIVE BARROW
          THEY IGNORED YOU AGAIN. THESE POLICE.

                    PROSECUTOR CORIC
          OBJECTION YOUR HONOR! DRAINERS IN THE
          POLICE INTERROGATION ROOM ARE STANDARD
          ISSUE AND TOTALLY LEGAL. THEY ARE AN
          INTEGRAL PART OF THE OFFICER'S ARSENAL
          AGAINST PERPS WITH A HIGH FLIGHT RISK,
          LIKE MR. MILLS.

                    JUDGE ROLLINS
          SUSTAINED.

                    DEFENSE ATTORNEY CLIVE BARROW
          LET ME ASK YOU, TOMMY, DID YOU FEEL WHILE
          YOU WERE SITTING UNDER THE DRAINER, THAT
          YOU WERE BEING QUESTIONED IN A SITUATION
          IN WHICH YOU COULD CLEARLY, AND TO THE
          BEST OF YOUR ABILITIES, HELP THE
          DETECTIVES IN THEIR QUEST?

                    TOMMY MILLS
          NO. NO, NOT AT ALL.

                    DEFENSE ATTORNEY CLIVE BARROW
          IN YOUR OPINION, IS THIS THE MAGAZINE
          ARTICLE YOU MENTIONED COMING BACK TO
          HAUNT YOU ALL OVER AGAIN?

                    TOMMY MILLS
          THE THOUGHT DID CROSS MY MIND.

CONTINUED: (17)

PROSECUTOR CORIC
OBJECTION!

DEFENSE ATTORNEY CLIVE BARROW
NO FURTHER QUESTIONS YOUR HONOR.

JUDGE ROLLINS
MR. MILLS YOU MAY STEP DOWN. BAILIFF? I
WOULD LIKE TO SEE COUNCIL IN MY CHAMBERS.
WE'RE GOING TO TAKE A RECESS UNTIL
TOMORROW MORNING AT 10 AM. EVERYONE HAVE
A GOOD NIGHT AND WE WILL SEE YOU
TOMORROW.

JUDGE DISMISSES JURY.

PARTIAL TRANSCRIPT FROM COURT DOCKET 55673-2433 THE PEOPLE
VS. THOMAS MILLS.

DATED 10:14 am October 23, 2001

JUDGE ROLLINS (CONT'D)
LADIES AND GENTLEMAN OF THE JURY, IT IS
MY REGRET TO INFORM YOU THAT THIS TRIAL
HAD ENDED. LAST NIGHT IN HIS HOLDING
CELL, THE ACCUSED, TOOK HIS OWN LIFE IN A
VIOLENT MANNER. THIS, OF COURSE, ENDS THE
PROCEEDINGS AND NULLIFIES ANY JUDGEMENT
YOU WERE TO BRING FORTH. I HOPE YOU WILL
ACCEPT MY SINCEREST APOLOGIES FOR THE
WASTE OF TIME THIS HAS BECOME FOR ALL OF
US- BUT I DO DECLARE YOUR DUTIES TO THIS
COURT COMPLETED. CASE DISMISSED.

JURY IS DISMISSED. 10:22 am October 23, 2001

POWERS
COLORING/ACTIVITY BOOK

**THE FOLLOWING PAGES ARE
FROM AN ACTUAL COLORING/
ACTIVITY BOOK**

**WHEN YOU VISIT THE POLICE
STATION IN POWERS, THIS IS
THE COLORING BOOK THEY
WOULD GIVE THE KIDS.**

POWERS
COLORING/ACTIVITY BOOK

Image

1.50
2.25
CANADA

POWERS

SAFETY KID

I, _____ , promise to use caution and safety everywhere I go. I will remind my relatives and friends how important it is to use safety all day long because this world is filled with super-powered maniacs and assorted radioactive menaces hellbent on destroying the Universe. So I will look both ways before I cross the street, always use a safety belt, and never touch anything in my house that has the word 'NULLIFIER' written on it.

_____

WRITE YOUR NAME HERE

_____   _____

DATE   **AGE**

image® COMICS PRESENTS:

JIM VALENTINO	Publisher
BRENT BRAUN	Director of Production
ERIC STEPHENSON	Director of Marketing
TRACI HALE	Controller/Foreign Licensing
BRETT EVANS	Art Director
ALLEN HUI	Web Developer
SEAN O'BRIEN	Inventory Controller
CYNDIE ESPINOZA	Accoutning Assistant

POWERS

CREATED BY
BRIAN MICHAEL BENDIS
AND MICHAEL AVON OEMING
COLOR ART LETTERING AND PRODUCTION BY
PAT GARRAHY

BUSINESS AFF
ALISA BEN

WORD SEA
MELISSA APON

IT'S TIME
TO PLAY...

FIND THE

SUPER

VILLAIN!

WORD SCRAMBLE!!!
FIND ALL TWENTY WORDS HIDDEN
IN THE GRID BELOW. WORDS MAY
BE FORWARDS, BACKWARDS,
HORIZONTAL, VERTICAL, OR
DIAGONAL. GOOD LUCK!

WORDS TO FIND:

1. HERO
2. VILLAIN
3. HEMPSTEAD ACT
4. DRAINERS
5. TRIPHAMMER
6. ZORA
7. COSTUME
8. REWARD
9. RETRO GIRL
10. DIAMOND
11. REPORT
12. MANIAC
13. SAFETY
14. STRANGER
15. ALTER EGO
16. SECRET IDENTITY
17. POWERS
18. CHESHIRE
19. POLICE
20. DANGER

L	I	V	E	R	D	E	G	G	B	S	W	Q	X	Z	K	A	C	Y
R	C	O	P	A	D	S	H	T	R	O	P	E	R	L	U	M	B	J
I	M	Z	X	C	A	Q	I	F	D	O	E	N	I	T	B	I	T	D
G	N	V	O	W	A	D	C	R	E	G	N	A	D	R	V	D	D	O
O	A	V	X	W	E	I	U	Y	F	R	W	E	C	I	L	O	P	S
R	Q	B	N	N	O	R	E	D	E	C	I	V	Q	P	U	L	P	B
T	U	E	T	R	E	T	I	Y	N	U	I	O	A	H	P	A	S	D
E	A	I	S	P	X	P	B	H	D	T	D	L	J	A	N	E	T	N
R	T	S	O	Q	A	W	C	V	S	Z	T	O	R	M	V	N	G	E
Y	R	R	C	R	I	M	E	H	E	E	R	M	R	M	A	P	W	V
T	I	E	R	O	D	I	R	T	R	B	H	O	U	E	B	A	B	I
H	P	N	C	U	M	E	R	E	K	R	P	C	C	R	R	C	U	T
G	L	I	F	U	G	C	G	D	W	E	E	R	K	D	E	P	M	C
I	L	A	M	N	P	O	W	E	R	S	J	G	E	P	L	N	S	A
F	G	R	A	F	T	T	R	H	O	W	D	D	N	O	M	A	I	D
I	T	D	N	H	O	E	N	F	A	B	I	A	T	A	F	G	A	A
N	S	T	I	I	R	N	R	L	I	C	E	S	T	E	R	W	O	E
N	W	E	A	R	B	T	W	C	E	N	I	N	T	D	E	T	C	T
R	E	D	C	O	U	R	A	G	E	O	U	Y	B	R	S	U	S	S
E	E	R	C	A	L	I	F	R	M	S	L	I	E	S	T	I	C	P
X	P	V	I	L	L	A	I	N	U	I	A	P	W	L	I	D	C	M
O	U	S	I	D	O	E	L	I	T	C	O	U	A	S	T	H	G	E
U	I	K	R	R	E	D	F	O	S	R	X	J	R	U	M	P	E	H
O	V	E	E	R	T	H	L	A	O	Z	Y	B	E	R	O	W	N	S
O	G	H	G	P	A	O	C	P	C	S	A	R	O	Z	S	D	I	O

USE COMMON SENSE AND
BE CAREFUL IN AN EMERGENCY.
SOMETIMES, SCARY THINGS HAPPEN.
IF YOU KNOW WHAT TO DO, HELP
IS JUST A PHONE CALL AWAY!

TRY TO STAY VERY CALM.
PICK UP THE PHONE AND DIAL 9-1-1.
WHEN THE OPERATOR ANSWERS, SPEAK
CLEARLY AND LOUD ENOUGH SO HE OR
SHE CAN UNDERSTAND YOU.
TELL THE OPERATOR THE NATURE OF
THE EMERGENCY.
ANSWER QUESTIONS, AND DON'T HANG
UP UNTIL YOU ARE TOLD TO BY THE
OPERATOR!

BE READY TO
GIVE THE OPERATOR
THE FOLLOWING
INFORMATION.

YOU CAN
FILL THIS OUT
AND KEEP IT HANDY
IN CASE OF A REAL
EMERGENCY!

MY NAME:

MY ADDRESS:

MY PHONE:

MY AGE:

WHAT'S THE NATURE OF THE EMERGENCY:

ARE SUPER-POWERED BEINGS INVOLVED:

911 MEANS *HELP* IS ON THE WAY!

MALL OUTING
A.K.A. KEYS

THIS IS THE FIRST EVER
BENDIS/OEMING COLLABORATION

THIS FIRST APPEARED IN A
BOOK CALLED 'JINX: TRUE
CRIME CONFESSIONS.'
IT IS PRESENTED HERE FOR
POWERS COMPLETISTS AND
CURIOUSITY'S SAKE

outing: mall

WELL, I'M A SOCIAL WORKER. SO THE STORY I'M ABOUT TO TELL YOU IS SADLY VERY, VERY PAR FOR THE COURSE...

THESE SHENANIGANS START IN A DEPARTMENT STORE.

LIKE A DILLARD'S OR SOMETHING...

ANYWAY, THIS LADY—THIS LADY IS WITH HER EIGHT YEAR OLD SON...

AND SHE IS SCREAMING BLOODY MURDER AT HIM..

SHE'S SHAKING HIM AND EVERYTHING...

SO THE KID ALSO STARTS SCREAMING AND CRYING...

REAL BLOOD CURDLING SCREAMING...

SHIVERS UP YO SPINE STUFF.

SEVERAL CLER AND EMPLOYEES TO CALM THING DOWN, BUT IT ALREADY OUT CONTROL.

SO, THEY'RE LEFT NO CHOICE...

THEY ESCORT HER AND THE SCREAMING KID OUT OF THE STORE AND INTO THE PARKING LOT.

INSIDE THE STORE, ANOTHER KID, THIS ONE IS A LITTLE OLDER, LIKE TEN...

STARTS STUFFING HIS SHIRT FULL OF STUFF!

A JACKET FULL OF STUFF...

EXPENSIVE CLOTHES, A WATCH...ALL KINDS OF...WHATEVER HE COULD GET IN HIS SHIRT...

Y'SEE?

SHE WAS PULLING THE OLD DISTRACTION BIT.

SHE MADE A SCENE.

ALL EYES ON HER.

THE KID GOES TO TOWN.

BUT THE SECURITY CAMERAS ARE ALL OVER THIS KID, SO THEY CALL IT IN.

A STATE COP WAS IN THE AREA, SO...

THE OLDER KID MEETS UP WITH THE MOM.

AND THE COP IS ALREADY YELLING OUT TO THEM.

BENDIS INTERVIEW

Interview by Alex Hamby
March 27th 2002

Alex: I'm a big fan of Powers. Where did that idea come from?

Brian: It's hard to put a thing on it...

It was a mixture of Mike [Oeming] and me becoming better friends through the years. He'd always show David Mack and I these drawings he was doing. He started doing drawings in the Powers' style of Kabuki, Jinx and Goldfish because that's what we were working on at the time. They excite both of us but they excited me to such a degree that I couldn't even stand it. At the same time I started analyzing why it was that I never attempted to write a superhero comic but I loved them so much. I really loved the genre – and I realized that a lot of my generation of comic writers, if you weren't assigned on of the heroes, Dark Knight and Watchmen kind of screwed it up for us.

We were raised on the ultimate [not to use Ultimate without getting a royalty] superhero stories in Dark Knight and Watchmen. It's sort of like everything had been said. So, I just moved onto another genre where I thought I had something to say. Then here we come, years later, and I analyze what I like about the genre and what I would have to say about it. I started thinking about the VH1: Behind the Music look at superheroes. Then I started mashing together my love of crime-fiction, love of the police procedural – then I started thinking about what the police procedure would be for superheroes but really get into it.

I had just read Homicide, the book that the TV show is based on, which is an amazing procedural. Then Mike started doing drawings, then I told him the idea and then he started doing drawings based on the idea. Then BOOM you got the whole thing.

Then I read Janice Joplin's biography and for some reason that made it click. I can't tell you why.

Alex: Ah, you're a Janice Joplin fan. We've got something in common. How do your goals differ from Powers and all of your other work?

Brian: They don't. Anything with my name on it has the exact same goal, which is to craft a book that I would buy. That's the goal. My personal goals are very very high. Higher than anyone has got for me, be it my employers or my readers. If my name is on it – There are very few things in this world that you get to leave behind just read Gil Kane's biography and I'm sitting there going, "You know what, man? There are very few things that will outlive you and comics will outlive me." Clearly we see that they will.

So, kick ass on them. At least make them something you would buy. People will like them, not like them, at least make sure that you will buy them. So, every decision I've made, jobs I take, that's the first test. Would I buy this book? Would I buy Daredevil with Alex Maleev drawing it? Hell yeah! Absolutely.

That's the goal.

As far as Powers is concerned, the only difference is that we get to kill everybody. We get to kill anyone we want whereas that is the one thing we wouldn't be able to do at Marvel. Marvel's not going to let me do a homicide book where I get to kill Captain America. So, we get to analyze the genre from that unique perspective.

Alex: You went through that whole starving artist thing.

Brian: Nine years of it thank you. [laughter]

Alex: You did a lot of stuff that people are retroactively talking about.

Brian: I don't care when they bought it as long as they bought it.

Alex: What do you think finally sparked the attention of Todd McFarlane and then Marvel?

Brian: Well, I actually know this. I was at Image and I had been there for many years before the founders even knew there was an Image central.

We all got comps. Todd was at Top Cow, saw the Goldfish trade and took it. He read it on the way home to Arizona. When he got back he said to Beau Smith, "Hey, find me this guy I think he's at Image." [Laughs]

He just really liked Goldfish, he really liked that kind of storytelling and he offered me a couple of projects. He goes, "I got two projects for you. One is a modern day Frankenstein..."

And I'm like, "Is this really Todd McFarlane on the phone?" It was really surreal, right?

"...it's about a giant monkey robot..." I don't want to do a giant monkey robot book.

Then he goes, "My other one's about two detectives." That sounds good! Then we started talking about Sam and Twitch and it was right up my alley. It wasn't a Spawn book and it was something I could do. That worked out real well.

Exactly at the same time, my friend David Mack started working at

Marvel Knights with Joe Quesada. I was absolutely in love with Marvel Knights, what it meant, what they were trying to do and how they were treating David. I think David slipped them a couple, I think, Jinx — and I think Joe just loved Jinx. Loved my writing, not my drawing, which he made very clear.

He called me — you get the Marvel Knights call, which is, "If you came to Marvel what would you do?" And I laundry listed stories I've been writing in my head since I was eleven. We were going to do Nick Fury but that didn't work out. Then Daredevil became a scheduling mess and he asked if David and I would do Daredevil. I was like, "Er, yeah...ok."

That was a book I was actually scared of. It meant so much to me i my youth that I didn't know. But I had a story I had been working of for quite a while and to work with David also was very important t me. David and I have been best friends since we both got into com and I wanted one time for us to do something worthy of that friendship. So, that was a very personal thing for me.

Then I literally handed in Daredevil scripts and that day Bill Jemas had plopped into Joe's office and said, "Gee, we've been working on this Ultimate Spider-Man but it's not coming together. Who wou you hire?" And shockingly Joe said me. We took it from there.

Joe calls me and says, "You're going to get a call to start Spider-Ma over again.

Alex: So, it happened all because you took on Daredevil?

Brian: If anything this says — and we're talking nine years into my comic book career this is happening — It's literally being in the right place at the right time. Finally one of my trades is on someone's desk at the right moment and finally I handed in a script and I was on someone's mind at the time when something I was qualified to do came around the pike.

I get this email everyday, every hour, that's like, "Help me. I can't break in."

I'm like, "Dude, I'm the last person to ask." I mean I Forest Gumped my way through this like no one's business. I am eager to be here and I am so happy but meanwhile I sent in 4,000 submissions between the age of 20 and 25 — I just stopped. I thought no one's interested. It's a lottery anyhow. Finally someone who could do something put me on a book like that.

It was fun and I didn't get fired right away, which I assumed was going to happen. So that was fun too.

I handed in a script for Ultimate two days after I got the gig. There was no Spider-Man, there's no costume. Either they're going to shit on this or they're going to love it. Thankfully they loved it or I woul have been kill-feed me, you would have never heard my name agai

Alex: Here's the ego question: Do you think your taking the Marvel gig led to the company's regaining some of the momentum it had lost?

Brian: I think decisions like hiring people like myself, David, Paul Jenkins and Straczynski — there's a thought process there that I am very proud to be a part of. I am one of a few things that worked out pretty well. My goals are pure and so are those of my friends who I just mentioned. We all just want to make really good comics with a unique voice. People really wanted that.

David and I kinda joke that we had to wait till everyone else left comics before we got our shot. Everyone from the early nineties left. They made their money, or they didn't, and they left. We stayed because we were going to stay either way. I would have just made my black and white comics and I would have been fine. So, we finally got our shot because there was nobody else left to hire.

I don't think it's me but I think there's a decision making process that is very forward thinking. I like working for forward thinking people. I like it in comics, when I'm working on stuff outside of comics — I like it when people are thinking outside the box.

Alex: Here's a long one: Now that you are with Marvel doing Alias, Daredevil, Ultimate Spider-Man and you're producing a Spider-Man cartoon, are you an independent writer working for a mainstream company or a mainstream writer who happens to do an indy comic in the form or Powers?

Brian: I run a company and one of the services that I provide Marvel is a big client for. Jinxworld is a company and it produces Powers and out of there comes my work for Marvel.

It's really weird because I don't put labels on any of this stuff. I treat it all the same. Just because it has my name on it, it has to be treated as if it's the last book I am going to get to write. As if it is the only shot I am going to get at this. I give it everything I've got.

I don't care about all of this other stuff. What I care about is the fact that one of these books will be the first book that someone picks up — of mine or of comics.

Alex: Good answer.

Brian: I don't want it to suck. Even if you don't like it you can at least say it's an interesting decision process. It's not my cup of tea but at least I can see the people behind it gave it shot.

Alex: Now, with working on so many books, how do you manage to give them each a unique voice?

Brian: A) I don't drink. [Laughs] There are traps of this business that I've learned wisely from the generation before me.

I have always admired and respected the work of people who

produced a lot of work like Jack Kirby and John Romita. I think that them producing a lot of work made the work a lot better. I think that when they were using all of their steam, it wasn't the volume of the work that mattered it was the quality that mattered. I alway aspired to be that kind of comic creator. On the same note, I don't want to be "Oh look he can write 50 titles". I have no interest in being that guy. It's just I can.

So, I don't drink and I don't play video games, which is the more horrible thing to happen to mainstream comics — the creation of Playstation. If they would take them away from comic creators you wouldn't even hear about a late book.

So, there's that and I am way way ahead of schedule. I am six months ahead on all of my books. That means whatever mood I'm in when I wake up, that's the book I'll write. There's no deadline emergency. If I wake up and I'm in a Daredevil mood — Usually when the book comes out and Alex [Maleev] and I are talking I am in a Daredevil mood, I'll write Daredevil because I'm in a mood to write it. I can be in a Powers mood for two solid weeks and write tons of it.

Alex: So, how long does it take you to turn out a book?

Brian: I don't know. Sometimes it takes a long time and sometimes you have a creative orgasm and it comes out of you. Not to be gros but sometimes it comes out of you. Don't you ever get to typing an you know, it just builds and comes right out of you. I don't know, it just very organic. When the organic thing's happening it's a lot of fu

Sometimes I type something that ends up looking like an Alan Mo script. Then I go back on a day when I am less of a fanatic and I format it so it looks normal. [Laughs]

That's the thing. If you stay ahead of schedule deadline is not an issue. It's all pure. So, anytime I have to write something under a crunch, I always hate it. I just don't want that feeling. That's just spoiling myself but it works for me.

Alex: Let's switch gears. This will be where things turn a little bit. I read in the back of an issue of Powers where you spoke about continuity. It was a transcript from a convention where you spoke about continuity. Can you give me a couple highlights regarding you beliefs regarding continuity?

Brian: What did I say? [Laughs]

Alex: Alright, I'll tell you. I can't quote it verbatim, I'll just get the basic jist...

Brian: Yeah, fine.

Alex: Your idea regarding continuity was respect for creators who came before you; that you didn't want to contradict someone else's work.

Brian: Yeah.

Alex: So, you hold true to that statement?

Brian: Yeah, pretty much. That's not the only thing but yeah.

Alex: I would think that this comes from the fact that the comic industry, as a standard rule, treats itself like a mini-Hollywood.

Brian: Not really. It may be perceived that way by you but a lot of the people I know in comics don't treat it like the be all end all of human existence. They are so happy to be doing comics.

Alex: Errrr...

Brian: I know. There are people in this business but they come and go so quickly that they don't even count to me. They are making properties so they can sell them. That sort of stuff.

Alex: But there are people in the industry who still act like that. We've been in and around the industry since the 90's. There's still that fan perception of creators thinking they are above the fans.

Brian: Are you saying that there are comic creators who act above the fans?

Alex: Yes. There's a lot of them.

Brian: There are a few of them. I would call those people assholes. Let's refer to them as assholes and there are assholes everywhere. That's not just in comics. That's everywhere! You leave the house and you're going to bump into an asshole.

There are people, say you walk around the small press alley, and

POWERS

NUMBER 13 • $2.95 US • $4.75 CANADA

BRIAN MICHAEL BENDIS • MICHAEL AVON OEMING •

ZORA'S BIRTHDAY GALA

EXCLUSIVE INTERVIEW
OLYMPIA
FROM GOLDEN ONE TO SCANDALOUS ONE

EXCERPTS FROM RETRO GIRL'S DIAR

IS IT REAL?   SCIENTISTS SAY THE DIARY MAY BE FAK

POWERS YOU DECIDE

RETRO GIRL'S WILD SEXY NIGHT WITH MYSTERY HUNK?

ZORA'S ANOREXIA NIGHTMARE

HOW SHE BEAT IT AND WHY?

POWERS

BENDIS OEMING

ge $2.95 US • NUMBER 14 • MATURE THEMES AND CONTENT

BUSTED!!

UPERHUNK OLYMPIA AND HIS SECRET LOVE AFFAIRS

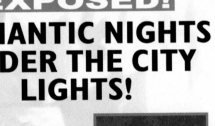

EXPOSED!

ROMANTIC NIGHTS UNDER THE CITY LIGHTS!

PLUS!

POWERS SCANDAL: THE SHARK LIED!!!

PECIAL BONUS SECTION

UPERPOWERS, FAME, AND MISERY...

GIANT SIZED
POWERS
ANNUAL

image

3.95
USA

BRIAN MICHAEL BENDIS
MICHAEL AVON OEMING

WE CAN TAKE ANY IMAGE + BREAK IT UP WITH SHARDS.
IVE ALSO DONE A PATCH ON THE ONE WITH BIG-JAWED
WALKER + PILGRIM LOOKING OUT WINDOW—
ILL DO THAT MULTI-PANELED ONE TOO.
—m

NEWSPAPER S.HOT.

MORE GREAT BOOKS FROM IMAGE COMICS

POWERS, VOL. 1:
WHO KILLED RETRO
GIRL? TP
ISBN# 1-58240-669-3
$21.99

POWERS, VOL. 2:
ROLEPLAY TP
ISBN# 1-58240-695-2
$13.99

POWERS, VOL. 3:
LITTLE DEATHS TP
ISBN# 1-58240-670-7
$19.99

POWERS, VOL. 4:
SUPERGROUP TP
ISBN# 1-58240-671-5
$21.99

POWERS, VOL. 5:
ANARCHY TP
ISBN# 1-58240-331-7
$14.95

GOLDFISH:
THE DEFINITIVE
COLLECTION TP
ISBN# 1-58240-195-0
$19.95

JINX:
THE DEFINITIVE
COLLECTION TP
ISBN# 1-58240-179-9
$24.95

FIRE:
THE DEFINITIVE
COLLECTION TP
ISBN# 1-58240-071-7
$9.95

TORSO:
THE DEFINITIVE
COLLECTION TP
ISBN# 1-58240-174-8
$21.95

TOTAL SELL OUT TP
ISBN# 1-58240-287-6
$14.95

ALSO AVAILABLE

40 OZ. COLLECTED TP
ISBN# 1-58240-329-5
$9.95

BAD IDEAS: COLLECTED! TP
ISBN# 1-58240-531-X
$12.99

CLASSIC 40 OZ.:
TALES FROM THE BROWN BAG TP
ISBN# 1-58240-438-0
$14.95

DIORAMAS, A LOVE STORY GN
ISBN# 1-58240-359-7
$12.95

BLOOD RIVER GN
ISBN# 1-58240-509-3
$7.99

WINGS OF ANASI GN
$6.99

KABUKI
VOL. 1: CIRCLE OF BLOOD TP
ISBN# 1-88727-980-6
$19.95

VOL. 2: DREAMS TP
ISBN# 1-58240-277-9
$12.95

VOL. 3: MASKS OF NOH TP
ISBN# 1-58240-108-X
$12.95

VOL. 4: SKIN DEEP TP
ISBN# 1-58240-000-8
$12.95

VOL. 5: METAMORPHOSIS TP
ISBN# 1-58240-203-5
$24.99

VOL. 6: SCARAB TP
ISBN# 1-58240-258-2
$19.95

NIGHT TRIPPERS GN
ISBN# 1-58240-606-5
$16.99

NOWHERESVILLE TP
ISBN# 1-58240-241-8
$14.95

THE FURTHER ADVENTURES OF
ONE PAGE FILLER MAN TP
ISBN# 1-58240-535-2
$11.99

GIRLS
VOL. 1: CONCEPTION TP
ISBN# 1-58240-529-8
$14.99

VOL. 2: EMERGENCE TP
ISBN# 1-58240-608-1
$14.99

GRRL SCOUTS
VOL. 1: TP
ISBN# 1-58240-316-3
$12.95

VOL. 2: WORK SUCKS TP
ISBN# 1-58240-343-0
$12.95

HAMMER OF THE GODS, VOL. 1:
MORTAL ENEMY TP
ISBN# 1-58240-271-X
$18.95

POWERS SCRIPTBOOK
ISBN# 1-58240-233-7
$19.95

PUTTIN THE BACKBONE BACK TP
ISBN# 1-58240-402-X
$9.95

QUIXOTE NOVEL
ISBN# 1-58240-434-8
$9.95

SAN AND TWITCH:
THE BRIAN MICHAEL BENDIS
COLLECTION, VOL. 1 TP
ISBN# 1-58240-583-2
$24.95

SIX GN
ISBN# 1-58240-398-8
$5.95

STUPID COMICS, VOL. 1 TP
ISBN# 1-58240-611-1
$12.99

ULTRA: SEVEN DAYS TP
ISBN# 1-58240-483-6
$17.95

WHISKEY DICKEL,
INTERNATIONAL COWGIRL GN
ISBN# 1-58240-318-X
$12.95

For a comic shop near you carrying graphic novels from Image Comics, please call toll free:
1-888-COMIC-BOOK

ERS

ODUCED BY
ND MIKE AVON OEMING

EDITOR
K C McCRORY

BUSINESS AFFAIRS
ALISA BENDIS

GROUPIES